G000093571

EAT LIKE
A LOCAL-
GRANADA

Granada Spain Food Guide

Zena Ballout

CZYK Publishing Since 2011.

Eat Like a Local

Lock Haven, PA
All rights reserved.
ISBN: 9798585335938

BOOK DESCRIPTION

Are you excited about planning your next trip? Do you want an edible experience? Would you like some culinary guidance from a local? If you answered yes to any of these questions, then this Eat Like a Local book is for you. Eat Like a Local - Granada, Spain by Zena Ballout offers the inside scoop and top tips on food and the best places to eat in Granada. Culinary tourism is an important aspect of any travel experience. Food has the ability to tell you a story of a destination, its landscapes, and culture on a single plate. Most food guides tell you how to eat like a tourist. Although there is nothing wrong with that, as part of the Eat Like a Local series, this book will give you a food guide from someone who has lived at your next culinary destination.

In these pages, you will discover advice on having a unique edible experience. This book will not tell you exact addresses or hours but instead will give you excitement and knowledge of food and drinks from a local that you may not find in other travel food guides.

Eat like a local. Slow down, stay in one place, and get to know the food, people, and culture. By the time you finish this book, you will be eager and prepared to travel to your next culinary destination.

OUR STORY

Traveling has always been a passion of the creator of the Eat Like a Local book series. During Lisa's travels in Malta, instead of tasting what the city offered, she ate at a large fast-food chain. However, she realized that her traveling experience would have been more fulfilling if she had experienced the best of local cuisines. Most would agree that food is one of the most important aspects of a culture. Through her travels, Lisa learned how much locals had to share with tourists, especially about food. Lisa created the Eat Like a Local book series to help connect people with locals which she discovered is a topic that locals are very passionate about sharing. So please join me and: Eat, drink, and explore like a local.

.

TABLE OF CONTENTS

DEDICATION

This book is dedicated to my beloved father who we lost too soon. He taught me the importance of fresh produce, flavours and spices; that food is a key instrument for bringing everyone together. My father was an exceptional cook, who never once used a recipe book, but preferred recipes passed down through generations and experimenting, always with incredible results. Everyone remembers his food, hospitable nature, and the rallying cry of "don't be shy!" to urge you to eat more. Thank you for your tips, advice, and encouragement. I would give anything to have you pretending not to hang around the kitchen (interfering) whilst I'm cooking again. And I agree, the best place for the tea towel is most definitely draped over the shoulder. Thank you for being my inspiration.

ABOUT THE AUTHOR

Zena is a British-Lebanese EFL teacher with nomadic tendencies who lives in Granada, ...but sometimes also in Manchester and Beirut. With a political science background, she has worked for NGOs in the Middle East, Africa, and Europe but eventually always ends up coming back to her love for languages.

Zena arrived in Granada to study a one month course, fell in love with the city, and decided to stay for a year. Afterwards, her absolute maximum one year stay somehow turned into 10 and counting...

A self-confessed foodie who loves cooking and trying out new recipes, with varying degrees of success, Granada is the perfect place for her to sniff out, quite literally, the freshest ingredients and bask in the Spanish culture's love for food and eating.

Travelling is another great passion of hers, as well as art, turning her home into a mini jungle, and learning about anything and everything. This combination of interests and curious nature often leads to inadvertent results: whether it be surviving being attacked by a mule; breaking ribs by coughing;

having cockroaches fall on her head throughout one horrifying night in Trinidad, Cuba; accidentally mistaking wasabi for pureed avocado; or unintentionally getting a ride back home through winding mountain roads with an armed militia, you could say adventure runs in her blood.

You can find her on social media - @oakandjazmin - where she makes, mostly futile, attempts at arts and crafts, humour, and addressing social justice issues in this wonderfully, chaotic world we call home.

HOW TO USE THIS BOOK

The goal of this book is to help culinary travelers either dream or experience different edible experiences by providing opinions from a local. The author has made suggestions based on their own knowledge. Please do your own research before traveling to the area in case the suggested locations are unavailable.

Travel Advisories: As a first step in planning any trip abroad, check the Travel Advisories for your intended destination.
https://travel.state.gov/content/travel/en/traveladvisories/traveladvisories.html

FROM THE PUBLISHER

Traveling can be one of the most important parts of a person's life. The anticipation and memories that you have are some of the best. As a publisher of the *Eat Like a Local*, Greater Than a Tourist, as well as the popular *50 Things to Know* book series, we strive to help you learn about new places, spark your imagination, and inspire you. Wherever you are and whatever you do I wish you safe, fun, and inspiring travel.

Lisa Rusczyk Ed. D.
CZYK Publishing

"You have to taste a culture to understand it"

- Deborah Carter

Granada is a traveller's absolute dream. There are very few places on the planet that can offer you beach, snowsports, and city life all in one. Making up a part of the southern Spanish region of Andalucía, Granada city is inland and doesn't quite get the same recognition as other southern cities such as the Andalusian capital Seville, and the coastal city of Malaga. However, those who miss Granada out on their itinerary are missing out on something truly magical.

Once ruled by the Moors for centuries, the influence of this reign is still noticeable today in all aspects of Granadino life. The architecture, craftwork, food, language, names of streets are all big giveaways, but the most obvious - the incredible Alhambra and the Albaicín (also spelt Albayzín) - are the jewels in this Granadino crown. My first year in Granada I spent walking everywhere thanks to my job which meant I got to know its streets and their secrets like the back of my hand. I quickly learnt how to become an honorary granadina, or granaína in the local dialect, and explored and discovered this city to my heart's content, and haven't looked back since. I promise you, in Granada, there really is something for everyone.

The city's beauty is evident from the outset, but it is all the small, underlying things, often missed by the tourists that go by on the tourist bus, that gives this special city its magic. I truly have Granada to thank for teaching me what is important in life through the simplistic pleasures it offers its inhabitants every day; walking through the Albaicín, watching the sun set from San Miguel Alto, the aroma of orange blossom hanging so pungent in the late-spring evening air to name just a few which all contribute to a love and passion for this city that I somehow can't leave.

"Every inquisitive traveller keeps Granada in their heart without having even visited it" - William Shakespeare.

I hope you enjoy this book and find the tips useful as they show you the real Granada as experienced through the eyes of a local.

Granada

Spain

Granada
Spain
Climate

	High	Low
January	54	36
February	56	38
March	62	42
April	67	47
May	77	54
June	87	62
July	94	67
August	92	66
September	83	59
October	74	53
November	61	43
December	56	37

GreaterThanaTourist.com

Temperatures are in Fahrenheit degrees.
Source: NOAA

1. THE POMEGRANATE CITY

In case you weren't aware, in Spanish, Granada means pomegranate. There are many theories about the origins of the name, which I won't go into great detail about here, but there is no denying that the pomegranate is a fruit that is held in high esteem in many cultures and traditions. Granada the city is no exception.

In areas surrounding the city there are pomegranate trees everywhere, noticeable for their bright orange flowers in the spring, and as autumn approaches, their infamous bright red skin. Most of the supermarkets and grocery shops in Granada sell pomegranates and they are likely to have been grown and picked from the surrounding area. How to eat a pomegranate? My top tip would be to roll the fruit on a hard surface or lightly tap the skin all over with the back of a spoon to loosen up the seeds inside before you cut into the flesh.

Granadinos are proud of their pomegranate and all it symbolises - look carefully, and you will find an image of a pomegranate almost everywhere in the city. On beautiful ceramic tiles and bowls, on the wall plaques of street names, on top of railings, even on the manholes on the city's streets! The humble pomegranate is also featured on the lower centre part of the emblem of the Spanish flag, representing the Kingdom of Granada.

2. TAPAS, TAPAS, TAPAS

You will have heard of the famous Spanish tapas, but the tapas of Granada take on a whole new meaning of the concept. In Spanish, the verb tapar means to cover and so the word tapa derives from this. Legend has it that originally a thin slice of bread or ham was used to cover the drinker's glasses of sherry in taverns to prevent flies from hovering over the sweet drink.

Tapas has now grown to new levels of recognition, featuring on menus around the world, they can be served hot or cold and vary greatly in quality and size.

Granada is famous for its tapas. On national public holidays that turn into long weekends, visitors from all over Spain come to Granada to experience its culture, magic, and tapas!

Basically, everywhere you go and order a drink, you will get free food. I'm not just talking a bowl of olives or a handful of nuts, no, proper food that you can actually dine off. Whether you order a beer, water, wine, or Coca Cola, you will get something scrummy to fill your tummy. Some places will bring you a tapa automatically with your drink, other places you get to choose what you order, usually with a maximum of two different varieties per table.

You pay the cost of your drink - anything from 1.70€ to 4€ - and the tapa is included. Some places you can get a good sized burger, others you can get typical dishes like paella and albondigas, meatballs in a tomato sauce. Take advantage of the huge amount of places just waiting for your custom, let your adventurous side take over as you delve into the glorious world of free food.

3. BIG TAPAS AND EXTRA TAPAS

Most places serve a good portion for tapas, but as with everything in life, there's always someone who has to go that one step further. These tapas may not be of the best quality, but they will certainly fill you up and for the price and the experience, you can't go wrong.

A hugely popular place is La Bella y La Bestia, yes, the Beauty and the Beast; the beauty being the fast service and the beast being the huge tapas. Found on Calle Carcél Baja near the Cathedral, and with another location on Carrera del Darro with views to the Alhambra, whilst traipsing around the main sightseeing spots, you're not going to be far from one. Perfect for when you need some powerfuel.

La Riviera on Calle Cetti Meriem, also near the Cathedral, offers large tapas which you can choose from the menu. A popular, busy place, you may need to wait for a table if you don't fancy standing by the bar. La Antigualla just off Plaza Nueva and its sister, just down the road on Calle Elvira also does large tapas and is usually a little quieter than La Bella y la Bestia and La Riviera.

One of my most favourites has to be La Sitarilla on Calle San Miguel Alta near Plaza de Gracia. Hugely popular with locals, and little known by tourists, it doesn't look like much from the outside, but inside it's like stepping into another world with quite large dining areas making way into other ones. The walls are decorated with the most incredible, large, colourful paintings of places in Granada, which, despite being inside without a view, casually keep reminding you that you're in one of the best cities in the world.

Top tip - get there early before the traditional Spanish lunchtime if you want a seat - the place is usually bustling, but it's well worth it.

4. CALLE NAVAS

Ah, Calle Navas, a place that is recommended in every travel guide and by tour guides alike. Of course, there is something to see and experience on Calle Navas and it is frequented by locals, but it could also be best described as a 'tourist trap'.

Would I recommend it? Not really. Unless you enjoy cramped together tables on a narrow street, lots of noise, shouting, and confusion. Add in a mix of young, international study-abroad kids being dragged on another bar crawl, and hordes of bachelor and bachelorette parties with random bits of paraphernalia of varying body parts near your face. Oh! And don't forget the odd poor little donkey riding through usually being silently crushed by an overweight, sweaty groom in a flamenco dress on its back. If that doesn't sound like your style - there are plenty of other areas and streets to explore and I will go into more detail on the next few pages.

5. BULLS AND TAPAS – PLAZA DE TOROS

To the northwest of the city lies Granada's bullring - Plaza de Toros. Bear with me now; as an animal lover, I vehemently discourage you from paying for and watching a bullfight, especially if you're then going to share on the 'gram the suffering and torture of an animal bleeding to death whilst being taunted. Not cool. Rant over.

However, the area itself is nice to see and has good links to the city centre. The bullring has nice architecture and the area is also known for its large tapas - that you can mostly choose from - making it popular with students. The actual bullring has many tapas bars underneath it built into the construction, but I would recommend El Nido del Búho, a popular spot with a grand variety of tapas at a low cost. Due to its popularity, you may need to wait for a table, but it will be worth it!

Another place worth a mention is La Nonna, a small, friendly, family-run Italian restaurant with some of the best dishes you will taste outside Italy. It is extremely reasonably priced for the quality. If you are travelling in a large group, you will probably need to book as the place is small. I guarantee it is a little hidden gem amongst the plethora of eateries in the area.

6. REALEJO

This area of Granada just off Plaza Nueva is like a tiny city in itself, full of life and with plenty to do. Formerly the old Jewish neighbourhood during the 8th to 15th century, Realejo is now home to many of the expats that live in Granada, as well as being home to the University's centre for studying Spanish, hence you will see a lot of study-abroad students in the area. This neighbourhood also has a great selection of places to replenish your worn-out batteries from walking around.

Café Bar Damasqueros on Cuesta del Realejo, is a friendly, relaxed place, with a lovely sunny terrace, albeit on a bit of a slope. In the winter they have a fire inside to warm you up whilst you sip a coffee after a crisp walk.

Pad Thai Wok on Plaza Fortuny serves decent Thai food where you choose everything from the type of noodles you want, the meat, the sauce, toppings, everything! Really nice food and a nice alternative to the usual offerings around.

Next to Pad Thai Wok is Papas Fortuny, a popular takeout place which serves baked potatoes roughly the same size as a small child's head with masses of toppings and sauce. Not quite what you're typically used to in the UK or other countries perhaps, but a nice alternative to the usual takeout as they serve until late at night.

Further into Realejo is the Campo de Príncipe, a large square with bars and restaurants surrounding it - especially popular with locals emerging for a stroll in the evening. Pull up a seat on one of the terraces and watch as the square comes to life.

7. CALLE ELVIRA

Running parallel to Gran Vía and connecting the Elvira Arch and Plaza Nueva, Calle Elvira may sometimes have a bit of a 'dodgy' reputation, and is known for being a bit grubby, but it is a must to experience on a trip to Granada.

The street itself is filled with tapas bars, Moroccan-style souvenir shops, and a lot of character. It was once one of the main streets in Granada and the buildings hugging it still hold the old Moorish style so commonly found in Granada. From this street you can really feel the change between the old Granada from the past, to the newer Granada of the modern day.

A great place to try is Bar Babel World Fusión, popular with locals and tourists, there is a good selection of unusual, tasty tapas to choose from - and vegetarians will be delighted that most of them are suitable for their requirements.

With it being such a bustling place, the service can be a little poor. However, while you're waiting you can be kept entertained by looking at the walls which are filled with portrait photographs of people from around the world, lit up by box lights. It's a nice touch and makes you feel warm and fuzzy looking at the beauty and variety of all these faces... but just to ever so slightly ruin the appeal - the images are actually a Google image search job as a friend of a friend visiting from the UK once horrifyingly found out when she saw her emo-esque MySpace profile photo proudly on display. Thanks, internet. Overall, a nice experience and you might even get lucky and spot your youthful mug beaming down at you reminding you of innocent days gone by before Zuckerburg et al. got the rights to your face.

Another fantastic place to try is Falafel Damasco, a small Syrian kebab shop, which might not look particularly appealing from the outside and you could easily walk past it, but trust me, this is some of the best falafel around. The place is more for takeaway, but as you wait for your kebab to be made, you will be given a freshly fried falafel ball topped with tahini sauce for free to keep you going. If falafel isn't your thing, try the pollo al tandori - tandori chicken kebab - which isn't hot spicy, but is flavoursome and so delicious that you'll want to repeat every day of your trip.

Word of warning: Calle Elvira is a narrow, one-way affair with cobbles and narrow pavements. There aren't massive amounts of traffic, but still, take care when walking along it, especially if you're unstable on your feet.

8. BARS, CAFES, RESTAURANTS

Ok, so these are three concepts that sometimes confuse the inquisitive traveller. In Spain, a bar is not a place to go and have only drinks on your night out; the beloved Spanish bar is like a sized-down version of a restaurant. Open almost all day, the bars are places you can go and get breakfast, lunch, tapas, a light dinner, and coffee, and are usually open until around the same time as restaurants - 11pm to midnight.

Cafeterias serve hot drinks, breakfasts, and even alcohol, but not usually larger meals - think a small sandwich, snack, or a piece of cake.

Finally, restaurants are like any other restaurant in the world, but usually open later until around 1am.

To add to all the misunderstandings, there are also places which promote themselves as cafeteria-bars, so basically a mix of the first two where anything goes. You don't need to get yourself too wound up about it all - all of them serve food and drinks, just if you're looking for a night out, the Spanish bar might not be what you quite had in mind.

In this case, what you're looking for is a discoteca, not to be confused with a club, which might cause an unceremonious end to your trip if you're travelling as a couple.

9. TYPICAL DISHES

There are many dishes in Spain which are famous the world over - Paella, Chorizo, and Gazpacho, to name a few. In Granada you will find typical, national dishes on offer, as well as many more local to Andalucía. One of my favourites and really sought-after in Granada, is patatas a lo pobre - poor man's potatoes - which is anything but poor. A really simple dish of sliced potato, green and red peppers, onion and garlic slowly fried together - sounds unimaginative, but that is the beauty of it - 'poor' ingredients, but packed full of flavour.

Another popular dish is migas, literally, breadcrumbs. Fried with bits of meat, peppers, and whole cloves of garlic with the skin still intact. A popular dish served as a tapa, but can also be found on the menu in restaurants.

Something else to try and a real treat for Granadinos is Pastel Moruno, a Moroccan-influenced pastry with a savoury-sweet sensation all at once! The filling is chicken with raisins, pine nuts, onion and tomato, with a flavouring of cinnamon and cloves. The pastry is then covered in icing sugar and is served in slices like a cake. The best place to try this unusual concoction is the bakery López Mezquita, half way down Calle Reyes Católicos. Tell them how big a slice you want, as the price is per kilo, they will weigh it, then you pay. Now, all you have to do is take your 'cake' and eat it - just make sure you wipe around your mouth regularly to avoid having a white dusting framing your lips for the rest of the day.

For more typically traditional dishes try popular local places like La Cueva on Calle Reyes Católicos or Los Manueles located on the same street.

10. WHERE IS THE VEG?!

In the UK we eat quite a lot of vegetables - no plate is complete without your 'meat and two veg'. In Spain, there is definitely a noticeable absence of the mighty green stuff on the menu which is hard to comprehend when there is so much fresh, good produce around. Most main dishes of either meat or fish will be accompanied with fries and maybe some scraggy pieces of lettuce if you're lucky.

If you're missing the healthy leaves from your diet, your best bet are the salads which are always fresh and wholesome; pisto, which is similar to the French ratatouille, except the vegetables in pisto are all cooked together; or fried vegetables, usually eggplant and zucchini, which are usually cut into strips and deepfried. Tomates aliñados is another simple, but delicious dish of bright red tomatoes chopped up and marinated in only the best olive oil, salt, garlic and fresh parsley and oregano. Also, the soups, or cremas, are usually packed with delicious vegetables with nothing else unusual added.

If you're vegan the mixed salad may have tuna or a boiled egg on top, so be sure to ask before you order.

11. THE MOST IMPORTANT MEAL OF THE DAY

Breakfast! I hear you cry - WRONG! In Spain the most important meal of the day is, without a doubt, lunch. This sacred time of day is when many shops in Granada may close their doors for a few hours and bars, restaurants and terraces fill to the brim with eager, hungry locals. If you choose to eat at the typical Spanish lunch time, expect to wait for a table and that the service may be a little slower due to the sheer demand for some delicious grub.

Like most Mediterranean places, the Spanish prefer to eat a larger quantity for lunch and then something smaller in the evening. Don't let this put you off eating what you want, when you want. Granada is used to tourists so you will have no problems in getting just a sandwich for lunch and something bigger in the evening, the choice is yours!

12. KITCHEN TIMES

Now, this is really important - especially for those of you who like to eat early! Granada is pretty strict on eating times, as in there is a specific time when to eat and kitchens fully close in the middle of the day which means no food for you, Señor!

As a general rule of thumb, most restaurants serve lunch between 12 and 4pm - the most popular time for the Spanish being from 2pm. Most restaurant kitchens close from 4pm to around 7/8pm when they reopen for dinner. Some do open a little earlier to accommodate the tourists, but the Spanish usually have dinner from 9pm onwards up until around midnight. The key hours between 4 and 8pm could be referred to as the infamous siesta time, which equals kitchen closed, even for tapas. Of course, there are some places that are open all the way through, and takeaway places will also be open in your time of need.

Breakfast places such as cafeterias open from as early as 7am, so you won't have a problem if you go by the 'first, coffee' way of life, and usually serve until around 11am or some places even until 12pm.

13. TAKEOUT AND APPS

The Spanish are extremely sociable beings and love nothing more than going out to eat in good company. However, no one can say no to a takeaway, and with the Coronavirus pandemic, more places have had to adapt and start providing takeout or having it delivered via an app.

Many places deliver the food themselves, you just need to call and place an order. If you don't speak Spanish, this might be a teeny-weeny issue. Luckily for you, there are delivery apps you can use which can help sort all that out so you can look through all the choices at ease knowing you don't have to speak a word of the lingo to not die of starvation. The most popular ones here in Spain are Justeat and Glovo - you can find the links at the end of the book.

14. MENÚ DEL DÍA

If your budget is tight, but you want to eat like a King, then the Menú del Día, or Menu of the Day, is for you! For a 3-course meal, usually with a drink included as well, you pay as little as 9€ to 15€ per person. You get to choose your starter, main, and dessert and the dishes are almost always traditional and delicious. If you don't speak Spanish, most places have the Menú del Día translated into English. The dishes are usually packed to the brim so if you get the Menú del Día for lunch, you're unlikely to want to eat for the rest of the day!

15. SIN PA'

Sin Pa' is basically a shortened version of the Spanish sin pagar (without paying) or in other words, bolt before you have paid the bill in a restaurant or bar. This is a custom that is mostly carried out by the city's youth, but is highly discouraged.

Often the service may be slow in Spanish restaurants and you can't seem to grab the attention of the waiter for the life of you - even enacting the universal squiggle with the index finger and thumb in the air trick doesn't seem to work. The temptation to just get up and leave in a huff is real and it almost consumes you - it's little wonder that people end up doing a sin pa' out of both frustration and pure desperation. However, if caught, you could land yourself in serious trouble with the local police and you would be lucky to be given just a hefty fine.

If you find yourself in this situation, make a big show of getting up to leave, putting on coats, grabbing bags, etc. and start to make your way over to the bar and someone will soon enough notice and give you the bill.

16. TIPS ABOUT TIPS

As a general rule in Spain, tips are around 10% of the bill. Many people don't give tips, or only do so after a meal, not tapas, a drink, or even breakfast. It is not usual for a service charge to be included in the bill. Giving tips is of course discretionary and very much depends on service, food quality, cleanliness, etc. And of course, each person's budget and standards.

However, I will say this; the waiting staff, chefs, and kitchen helpers are usually paid, quite frankly, an abysmal amount for working long, hard hours of often 12 hours daily. As well as barely getting any breaks during a shift and only one day off a week, most places are also noticeably understaffed. Please be patient. Many of the staff rely heavily on tips that are given to heavily supplement the wages they are given.

17. LOST IN TRANSLATION

Something to bear in mind - bad English translations here are very common in Granada. "Climb ants to the tree", anyone? How about a "tuna milkshake"?

Of course, these examples are some of the absolute worst which I don't even think the best linguists on the planet could make sense of. To avoid any upset, better to have a handy phrase book or phone app on hand ready to translate the Spanish so you won't get any nasty surprises when your food arrives.

18. SHOW ME THE DOUGH

Once upon a time in Spain, sliced baguette bread was served in cute little baskets whenever you ordered food, and usually demolished as you ravenously awaited your food (or is that just me?). Quite simply, bread is a staple accompaniment on the Mediterranean table.

However, things have changed. More often than not the bread is still brought out, but then when you get your bill at the end there suddenly appears a pesky little charge for some stale bread you either picked at reluctantly, or didn't even notice was on your table.

The cost can be minimal, maybe 50 cents per person, but sometimes it can peak to around 1.50€ which suddenly adds up to quite a bit on a family dinner if you didn't even order the wretched stuff.

If you see the waiter marching over ready to dump a basket of bread on your table, don't be afraid to say no, gracias; they won't bat an eyelid and will take it away ready to drop it like hot cakes on the next group of unassuming diners.

If like me you're all about the golden doughy stuff, you're going to loaf Pan de Alfacar. Hailing from the small Granadino village of, believe it or not, Alfacar, the bread is much beloved in the area. In 2013 it was given the prestigious title of Protected Geographical Indication product to recognise its traditional origins and quality by the European Union. The bread itself is like a long, flattened oval shape and can be found in most bakeries in the city. You can also find versions made with olive oil, and sweeter ones made with raisins and covered in sugar - the choice is endless!

19. TABLE ETIQUETTE AND DRESS

Granada has a student population of almost 80,000 which influences the general feel of the city and dress code. When going for tapas relaxed, laid-back attire is absolutely fine, even for most restaurants. There is another extreme when people go to eat in higher-end restaurants, usually around the Calle Ganivet area, where people dress up to the nines and you will feel very out of place with your comfortable walking shoes and rucksack. Dress smart casually, and you can't go wrong.

Only at restaurants will the table be laid and the usual table manners are expected. In bars, you will probably get your cutlery in a wrapped-up paper napkin and maybe a paper placemat if you're lucky. In places serving tapas, forget all that. The plates will arrive with small forks or spoons ready for you to dig right in with little expectation for manners and table etiquette.

Another thing to bear in mind is that many dishes are to be shared - even if you're getting a tapas each, they may all arrive on the same plate. Don't be shy! Dig in and relish the joy of communal eating.

A common sight on the Spanish eaterie's table is the small, square tissue holder ready to burst with little white grease-proof tissues - an absolute essential to the Spaniard's eating process. In many places you will see the tissues strewn on the floor and - environmentalists, look away now - locals merrily adding to the collection as they eat. A floor with a white spread after the lunch rush is a sign of a success both for the food, and the till. It might sound disgusting, and there will be someone frantically going round trying to sweep up the mess, but I promise it's a sign of a good, local place and not a sign of Iberian opposition to saving the planet.

20. NO-LIMITS ALCOHOL

If you drink alcohol, you may need to be aware of the, lets say, lack of measures in Spain. If you ask for a spirit, you will be served it in a spirited way, as in, there is no such thing as single, doubles, etc. The server will just keep pouring until they think a sufficiently large enough amount has been administered. Bear in mind that the glass is usually filled with a great big chunk of ice (if we were back in 1912, it could easily give the iceberg which hit the

Titanic a run for its money), and the alcohol is then filled over the iceberg which results in the glass being about two-thirds full of alcohol, with a small glass bottle of mixer on the side for you to add as much (or as little) as you'd like.

Chupitos, or shots, are also very popular in Spain and you are often served one at the end of a large meal after you have paid and given the choice of an alcoholic or non-alcoholic liquor. People are such fans of the mighty little shot that there is even a bar in honour of them called Chupetería 69, on Calle Sócrates, to the south of the city. There are over 100 shots to choose from varying from 'soft' to 'hard'. It's an extremely popular student place, but also frequented by people just passing by to see what all the fuss is about. As it is located right by Calle Pedro Antonio de Alarcón, which is full of nightlife, bars, and fun, it is easy to see why this place is so popular.

*Warning: alcoholic drinks here are super cheap compared to most other places in Europe and along with the strength of the drinks, drinking with caution is advised. Drunk and disorderly behaviour is heavily frowned upon in Spain and the police don't take too kindly to drunks rolling around and causing trouble after downing too much of the special brew, especially not foreigners.

21. WAYS TO PAY

Spain was very much a cash-only society in most places until very recently. As contactless payment cards and banking apps grow in popularity, the need to carry cash has declined. The Coronavirus pandemic has further pushed the desire for cash to the bottom of the pile.

That being said, I recommend you do carry money around with you as some smaller businesses and shops like kiosks don't accept cards. If your friendly customer agent in the bureau de change gave you a mound of 50€ notes, you might not think of them so amicably when most places say they can't take such a large note. Try if you can to get lower denominations of notes to make your life a lot easier.

In addition, it is not unusual for card machines to not be working at public transport payment stops, and you can't pay onboard for buses by card, so make sure you have some cash with you so you don't get caught out.

Also, it's always nice to carry around some loose change to leave as a tip - it will always be much appreciated!

22. TAKE YOUR TIME

That's right - take.your.time. Seriously, not in a peace and love, hippie sort of way, but in a live in the moment and enjoy your food and the company sort of way. There is no rush here in Granada, and when you sit down for a meal, you don't need to worry that another group of hungry folk are going to be arriving soon ready to be seated for their reservation. It is not uncommon for groups of people to spend hours and hours at a table taking their sweet time over every course of the meal, then coffee, then perhaps alcoholic drinks, mixed with non-stop chattering, then even start all over again with tapas. You won't see waiters hanging around nervously waiting for the revellers to move on, they'll just be there on hand to keep plying them with whatever takes their fancy next.

Sometimes the serving times may be slow, sometimes you may need to wait longer than expected for your bill, but this is all part of the spectacle of eating out in Spain. No amount of rage, insistence, or glares will change this attitude that is seemingly inbuilt into every Andalusian at birth. So, if you can't beat them, join them! Savour every mouthful of food, the atmosphere, take your time, and most importantly, enjoy the moment.

23. KIDS 'N' ALL

Spanish society is very much family-orientated and so the use of babysitters is almost non-existent. Children are just as important at any family gatherings and are included in meals out, no matter what the time. You will see children as young as 2 years old still happily tottering around at midnight while their parents and friends are engrossed in a conversation about jamón, football, how Spain is the best country in the world, or whatever other stereotypical subject you want to imagine.

This doesn't mean the children are off there on their own misbehaving, far from it. They're usually entertaining themselves doing kid things like looking at rocks, falling over, and hanging off a tree somewhere.

So, let your kids experience a world they're probably not used to at home, and you too, indulge yourself with a guilt-free night where bedtime routines are forgotten.

NB, I bear no responsibility for any bad moods and tantrums that may occur thanks to a late night after reading this tip.

24. IT'S NOT EASY BEING GREEN

Spain in general is only very recently coming around to the idea of vegetarianism and veganism, although I would say in a lot of cases, quite reluctantly. Don't be surprised if you order a vegetarian sandwich from the tapas menu and it comes with a great big slab of jamón (ham) thrown on top. When you order, you really need to emphasise you don't want ANY meat or fish on your plate, most places will understand, but some of the more traditional places you may get the incredulous, "what, not even chicken?!" barked back at you.

With the student population bringing with it more curious minds, vegetarian options are becoming more and more popular in Granada. There are plenty of legit vegetarian options on menus popping up including some places being extra adventurous and even using - shock, horror - tofu and chickpea based dishes, like falafel.

Restaurante Vegano Hicuri on Plaza de Gírones, not far from Plaza Nueva, is a vegan-only spot with a great selection of mains and desserts. The walls of the place are also adorned with some fantastic artwork which is similar to the street art seen in the Realejo area.

For another vegan experience, Restaurante Páprika just off Calle Elvira near the Arco de Elvira is a good choice for unusual, vegan-only dishes including organic and vegan wine and beer. The service can be slow and relaxed here, but the food is good and the terrace outside perched on a gentle hill allows you to sit back and watch all the hustle and bustle going on on Calle Elvira.

Calle Elvira in general is a good bet for more 'alternative' food and you won't be too hard pushed to find vegetarian and vegan options. Bar Babel World Fusión (see chapter 7 - Calle Elvira) is another great spot for deliciously green delights.

Awareness around allergens is becoming more prominent in Spanish restaurants which could also work in your favour when ordering a vegetarian dish.

25. SOME LIKE IT HOT... OR NOT

In general, Spanish food isn't spicy and it is hard to find hot, spicy food here - something which I know a lot of tourists complain about. There are a few typical dishes that do have a little fiery kick like patatas bravas, chorizo, and pulpo a la gallega - octopus done Galician style, which might have a little umph from the paprika used.

For hot spice you need to look for things on the menu which are picante. Spanish food is deliciously flavoursome, but this is from spices, not spicy - the most kick you will get is from food which contains a lot of garlic, paprika, and pepper. Gambas al Pil-Pil is another dish you could try as it uses plenty of garlic and a bit of red chili pepper. Another option is to take your chances with the russian roulette that is the pimientos de padrón. Order a plate of the small green fried peppers and see if you hit lucky. A famous expression that accompanies these potential tastebud annihilators is 'unos pican, otros no', basically; some are hot, others are not - and that's exactly how it goes.

26. GIVE A MAN A FISH AND FEED HIM FOR A DAY...

Granada's close proximity to the sea means that the city is flooded (ha!) with an enormous variety of good quality, fresh fish, normally found on the coast.

There are some real, quality fish and seafood places in the city, my absolute favourite being Los Diamantes, the Diamonds, and boy is this place a diamond. Not only do they serve decent sized tapas of fresh fish and seafood, the prices are excellent and average for the city. They have 5 sites across the city and are always bustling and full of life, and much loved by locals. The service is quick, despite the busyness, and the fish is always fresh and does not appear to have been fried in the same oil used for the past few hours as some other places are known to do. You may need to sit quite close to others and even share benches, but that is all part of the fun and appeal of this place. At typical Spanish lunchtime it can get extremely crowded, so be prepared to have to wait for a space. It can also get pretty noisy, but in a nice enjoying-life sort of Spanish way. Do order things off the main menu, if you like fish, you will die for the surtido de pescado - a mix of fried fish such as whitebait, fat, juicy prawns, squid rings, and dog fish. Trust me, you wont regret it!!

Just off Plaza Bib Rambla is the small square Pescadería, or fish square. It's a lively little square around eating times and with its location just below the Cathedral, has some excellent views. There are plenty of places to choose from here - some places can be a bit pricey, but definitely worth it. If your budget doesn't stretch quite that much, there are plenty of places in and around the square which offer the infamous Menú del Día at a fraction of the price of the more expensive ones. Places in the square usually have their menus chalked up on a board outside so it's easy to spot which ones offer the cheaper menu. The more expensive places usually have your future dinner bobbing about in a squashed up fish tank at the front of the restaurant, a great unintended aquarium attraction for kids, but probably best not to tell them where little Nemo may end up later on that evening…

Another recommendation for here is La Freiduría de Tere, a tiny little takeaway place at the end of the square where you can get cones of freshly fried fish to takeaway. The place is very popular so don't be surprised if they're closed when you get there because they have sold out. The opening hours are in the morning between 11am and 2:30pm, so it is most definitely a lunch option. I suggest grabbing your cone and sitting in the square or wandering down to Plaza Trinidad just a minutes walk away, or up to the Cathedral and sit on the steps in front of it to enjoy freshness and history all in one mouthful.

27. AFTERNOON TEA – SPANISH STYLE

After all that lunchtime eating you would think that more food and drink wouldn't be an option. That's why the glorious siesta is involved after lunch for you to rest, nap, and build up your energy ready for more local experiences. Once the Spanish emerge from any post-lunch food comas, they can commence the merienda, similar to an afternoon tea or snack.

On the menu now is coffee, cakes and sweet treats or the almighty chocolate con churros (see next chapter) and a whole lot of conversation and catching-up.

Another curious offering that you will see advertised around this time of day is café y copa - yes coffee and a drink in the form of a spirit and a mixer. Why you drink them at the same time is anyone's guess, but it's a popular pastime in Granada and many places offer the combination for as little as 4 or 5€.

28. CHOCOLATE AND DONUTS

One of the most famous sweet dishes in Spain is chocolate con churros, which can be best described as long, sugary donuts served with thick, gloopy chocolate served in a cup on the side. Some people choose to order a coffee with the churros and dip them into the warm liquid instead of dunking them into the chocolate - the choice is yours. Usually each person orders their preference of dipping beverage and then the churros are brought out on a plate (amount served depends on how many people are eating) and everyone just gets stuck in - don't be shy! This is quite a greasy, glutinous activity, but one that Spaniards feverishly take part in.

Served in places called churrerías, the preferred time to eat churros con chocolate is either for breakfast or to form part of the merienda or late evening from around 7/8pm.

The best place to try them in Granada is just off Fuente de Batallas, on Plaza de Mariana Pineda at Café Fútbol - yes, a football cafe - where you will be surrounded by memorabilia of Granada Football Club's trials and tribulations over the years. Alternatively, they have a lovely large terrace where you can watch the world go by whilst not feeling one bit guilty about how many calories you're pumping into your body as everyone else around you is doing exactly the same thing.

Another top location is on Plaza Bib Rambla where many locals flock in the evening to take part in this calorific mission, so you will be in good company. Many of the cafeterias surrounding the square have good quality churros, but I'd have to say the best, and an extremely popular spot with locals, is Cafetería Alhambra, which also has a nice terrace to sit outside and watch the square come alive with street performers, families out walking, tourists looking confused about where the Alhambra (the real Alhambra) could be.. You get the picture.

29. COFFEE, WITHOUT THE BUCKS

Like most Mediterranean countries, coffee is a big thing here. Whether it's a cortado (small espresso coffee) to guarantee you stay alert for the next few days; or a café manchado (literally, stained milk - stained with a dash of coffee that is) to make the coffee snobs snigger at your fragility; or the classic café con leche, you will find the coffee of your choice. The coffee is cheap - around 1.20€ maximum, no-fuss, and never disappointing. However, if you're looking for a large cup of the brown stuff, you may struggle as most coffees are served in an average-sized cup on a saucer.

In line with the absence of no big food chains in the city centre, Granada somehow managed to escape the arrival of Starbucks until 2018. Luckily, it is a fairly small one on Gran Vía de Colón, and most of the traditional cafeterias in Granada still remain strong and authentic, scattered proudly throughout the city.

As the warm weather arrives, the locals start to prefer a slight twist to their usual afternoon coffee and so you will see the café con hielo (iced coffee) arriving at their tables. A steaming cup of coffee will arrive with a large glass with an iceberg inside… pour the hot coffee over the ice and don't panic if half of it dribbles over the table - no one is good at this precarious act. Then sit back and enjoy a refreshing glass of cool coffee - bliss.

30. NOT YOUR TYPICAL SPANISH CAFÉ

As mentioned before, Granada has an abundance of your typical Spanish cafeterias. There are also a few hidden gems if you're looking for something a bit more alternative and more of a relax-and-get-lost reading your book sort of way. Bohemia Jazz Café has to be my most favourite, situated on Plaza de Los Lobos, and hidden behind an unassuming door lies a whole new meaning to the word 'eclectic'. The walls are adorned with framed images from Mike Tyson to Audrey Hepburn with soothing jazz sounds playing in the background; some days you might even find an elderly man tinkering on the ivories of the grand piano, not as a performance, but purely just for pleasure.

The place is cosy and feels homely and the servings are HUGE. The menu lists ice creams and coffees under the names of jazz related themes - think New Orleans, Paris Jazz, Blue Note. A real unusual spot if you want to get away from it all.

La Qarmita on Calle Águila near Plaza de Gracia is another popular place as it is not only a cafeteria but also sells a selection of books and holds events such as poetry nights and art exhibitions. Calling itself an alternative social space, their cakes and snacks are all homemade and they have over 30 different teas to try! A little further away from the usual sightseeing places, but definitely worth a visit.

31. TEA HOUSES

One thing you must do for a thoroughly Granada experience is go to a tetería, or teahouse. The atmosphere in these places is very relaxed and you can sit back and contemplate your day/trip/life to your heart's content in soothing surroundings usually accompanied by softly playing Arabic music or even the sound of a fountain.

To further induce your state of zen, the lighting is usually quite soft and low, but with bright colours being emitted from colourful glass lamps, which can also be bought in the shops nearby. On the menu is a selection of teas to choose from, milkshakes, and deserts like crêpes and ice cream. Take the chance to also try some traditional Moroccan sweets Chebakia - fried rose-shaped pastry soaked in syrup, or Middle Eastern Baklava - sugary, syrupy, thin sheets of pastry stuffed with nuts.

I recommend after paying a visit to El Mirador de San Nicolás, that you walk back down towards the centre and Gran Vía de Colón via Calle Calderería Nueva. The street was once home to a range of shops from DIY to local produce, but is now inhabited by teahouses galore and small shops selling beautiful trinkets. As you start to walk down the hill you will see the narrow street wind down before you with all the brightly-coloured fabrics and lights on display, making it a perfect photo opportunity.

32. PIONONOS

Possibly one of the most famous dulces (sweets) to come out of Granada is the small but mighty Pionono. The small cake was created in 1897 in a village just outside Granada called Santa Fe, where the airport also happens to be located. It is said that the cake was created in honour of the Pope Pio IX (pronounced pio noveno in Italian), hence the name Pio-nono. The shape of the Pionono is similar to that of a tophat, but without the rim and is said to represent the shape of the Pope's hat.

The sweet itself is, ahem, sweet. Very sweet. But absolutely delicious and an utter must to try when in Granada, not just for its historical significance, but also for its traditional, secret recipe that has been passed down through generations.

It is made of a fine sponge sheet which is moistened with syrup and filled with cream and cinnamon. This is then rolled up and put into an upright position where it is crowned with more cream and then toasted or caramelised to produce the most incredible flavour.

Although piononos can be found at most pastelerías (bakeries) throughout the city, the quality does vary quite significantly. I recommend purchasing a pionono at Casa Ysla, which has many cafeterias in the centre. Not only has Casa Ysla won many prizes for its Piononos, but it is also the home of the delicacy as the descendants of the creator, Ceferino Isla, continue to run the business today.

33. ICE CREAM IS ALWAYS A GOOD IDEA

In the sweltering hot summer days of Granada, there is nothing better than plopping yourself down on a bench in a square and devouring flavoursome ice cream, and luckily for you, there are plenty of ice cream parlours to choose from.

Many of the ice cream shops in Granada display their offerings in the most imaginative and photogenic way. Think massive pineapple wearing sunglasses shoved on top of pineapple flavoured ice cream with tiny paper sun umbrellas framing it - creative, amusing, and delicious all in one, what's not to love?!

By far the greatest and most famous is Los Italianos on Gran Vía de Colón. Taking centre stage in Granada since 1936 the ice cream is excellent and extremely reasonably priced for the quality and it is always busy with people eager for that ice cool hit of deliciousness. It is not uncommon for the place to be frequented by famous Spanish politicians, and even Michelle Obama, the wife of ex-U.S. President Barack Obama, and their daughters couldn't resist a visit to Los Italianos when they came to Granada in 2015. The shop has also opened up a small terrace at the back where there is table service and you can also grab a coffee. They have plenty of flavours to choose from, but my recommendation would be the cassata - in particular, the coffee one - a three flavoured-tiered ice cream in the shape of a piece of cake shoved into a thick wafer cone (or tub if you're not a cone fan). Even more excitingly for all you gelato fanatics, in the summer months the shop is open until midnight, so there really is room for dessert!

Just remember - Los Italianos is only open in the summer months between late March until October - the dates are never fixed and in the autumn months you can often see people walking away from the shop disappointed to find it has closed and instead in the window lies its infamous winter display of an elf getting to work ready for Christmas. When Los Italianos reopens its door in the Spring, there really is a feeling of excitement in the Granadino air that the longer days and warmer climate are on their way.

34. NON-ALCOHOLIC OPTIONS

Although the Spanish love their beer and wine, the culture isn't quite as focused on boozing as perhaps some other European nations, so it's perfectly easy to get immersed into Spanish life without the need for alcohol.

As well as the usual soft drinks of Coca Cola, Fanta, Sprite, etc. there is also the ever popular Nestea, a refreshing cold ice tea with a hint of lemon. Bottled still water and sparkling water are also popular, as well as mocktails of all the usual flavours.

There is also a drink called Mosto, which is grape juice in its purest form, before it is fermented to become wine, therefore making it non-alcoholic. The Granadino coastal town of Salobreña is famous for its own version of mosto called Castillo de Salobreña which is made with apple juice and either red or white grapes. The bottles can be bought in most supermarkets or ordered as a drink in a restaurant or bar.

If you don't drink for whatever reason, it truly is a breath of fresh air to be able to get a non-alcoholic drink after sunset and to not feel judged in the slightest!

35. PIZZA

When in Spain, why eat pizza one may ask. True, but sometimes pizza is one of those little comforts we all need when travelling, and Granada has some great options. Apart from the usual chains of Dominos and Telepizza, there are some other little gems I'm going to tell you about.

One of the absolute go-to pizzerias is Pizza Metro on Calle Gran Capitán, where, you guessed it, the pizza is a metre long!! They have plenty of flavours to choose from and if you do order a metre, you can have up to four different flavours or toppings on it to make sure everyone is satisfied. If having a metre of pizza doesn't appeal to you, not to worry! They also have 'normal sized' 9" and 12" pizzas and also slices and other dishes including salads and pasta. When you walk into the restaurant on the right hand side is a counter where you can choose a slice of pizza to takeaway or to eat sitting on the barstools there.

Another recommendation for pizza is Il Gondoliere on Calle Martínez Campos, which is popular with locals and definitely more of a place to dress up for and probably make a reservation for dinner. The restaurant has a takeout place, Il Gondoliere Espresso, on Calle Acero de Casino where there is the option to buy slices of their delicious pizza or pasta and eat in or takeaway - great if you need a quick snack whilst on-the-go.

36. THE ALHAMBRA

"I do not know what to call this land upon which I stand. If what is beneath my feet is paradise, then what is the Alhambra? Heaven?" - Lope de Vega

The most famous landmark in Granada and the most visited in Europe, there aren't sufficient words to describe the beauty, splendour and true magnificence of the Alhambra palace. I have never known a place which gives the same gasp-inducing wonder from both the inside and out. One of the best places to admire the building in all its awe-inspiring spectacle is from the Mirador de San Nicolás, opposite the Alhambra across the River Darro. Not only does this place offer spectacular views of the Alhambra, the city, and incredible sunsets, but there are also plenty of restaurants just below it with very reasonable prices which overlook the 9th century marvel in all its glory.

I would especially recommend going at night when the Alhambra is all lit up with a golden hue, but

I do recommend you make a reservation. During the day, sit on the terrace of one of the many restaurant patios just below the mirador to have a coffee and take in the view that beholds you.

37. FOODIE SHOPPING LIKE A LOCAL

Shopping in Granada for foodies is a joy, especially if you want to share your newly-discovered delights with family and friends back home. Head to around the Cathedral area of the city and you will find many shops selling traditional food products, and beautifully gift-wrapped items to either treat yo'self, or some other lucky devil.

The shops around display their tea and ground spices much like you see in the markets of Istanbul or Marrakech and you can buy per 100g at very reasonable prices. Some of the loose tea is fantastic, especially Té Pakistaní and Sueños de la Alhambra, or you can pick up some of your favourites you have tried in the teahouses. Most places also sell tea in a nice tin with the typical Islamic geometric pattern that Granada is famous for, which makes for a really nice souvenir.

Here you can also buy good, quality virgin olive oil from the local area and some places even sell small bottles of 100ml, which, with the limits on travelling with liquids, is great if you're travelling with hand luggage only!

You can also pick up locally produced honey, jam, and marmalade of all sorts of flavours from papaya, to apple and rose, to rosemary!

My advice? Go and spend some time strolling aimlessly through these shops and see what local delights you can find - you may overspend on your budget, but your tastebuds, senses, and gift-recipients will thank you for it!

38. SQUARES, VIEWS AND PEOPLE WATCHING

One of my most favourite things to do when travelling is people watch; a strange (some may say creepy) pastime, but for me, watching the world go by, the locals doing their thing, and learning about a new way of life, gives a unique insight into a place for the intrepid traveller.

I really encourage you to sit on some squares and take it all in, get your takeout kebab/coffee/ice cream/sustenance of choice and head to Plaza Nueva, Plaza Trinidad, or Plaza Bib-Rambla to name a few.

One of the most favoured by locals is Paseo de los Tristes, I say locals as many tourists struggle to find the area as on most maps and guides, its official name of Paseo del Padre Majón is used. Continuing from Plaza Nueva along Carrera del Darro towards the Albacyin will eventually lead you to Paseo de los Tristes, or 'way of the sad ones', named as such in the 19th century as it was the way towards the San José cemetery. This beautiful area sits in the shadow of the Alhambra and people sit on the walls overlooking the River Darro chatting and relaxing. There are a number of bars and restaurants here with large terraces with spectacular views of the Alhambra above; sit back, enjoy some good food, and be anything but sad in this wonderful environment.

39. HOLY DELIGHTFUL

The Catholic Church in Spain is still a prominent feature and its festivals and services still make up a great part of Spanish life. The grandeur of many of the chapels and churches throughout the city is enough to capture your attention, but little known to the unsuspecting traveller, there are many cloistered nuns living behind the closed doors making biscuits and sweet treats ready to sell. A box of the homemade sweets is around 6€, but the experience is priceless. One of the best places is Convento de Santa Catalina de Zafra on Carrera del Darro, just further on from Plaza Nueva, walking towards Paseo de los Tristes.

Just press the doorbell outside and wait a few minutes for the wooden door to open. You won't be greeted by anyone, nor will you see the nun who serves you, but go inside and request the type of biscuits you want (note: most won't be vegetarian!). Wait until the rotating table turns to reveal your box, put your money on the table - cash only! - and if necessary, your change will be returned in the same method.

Just be aware that nuns don't follow usual business hours so you might not get an answer the first time you go, go back later on and see if you have better luck. The biscuits also make great gifts as they come nicely boxed and make a great story that you've taken part in a tradition at a convent dating back to the 16th century!

40. WHY HAVE ABS WHEN YOU CAN HAVE KEBABS

Oh, how beloved is the greasy, stuffed-to-the-brim, hunger-demolisher, all-round winner, the humble kebab.

The clubs and late night bars in Granada usually wrap up at around 6am, yes, AM. This is usually followed by two options - food, or food - one being chocolate con churros, the other, our old friend the kebab.

The kebab, which sometimes also goes by the Arabic name, Shawarma, is an oval pitta bread packed with salad, falafel or meat in the form of either chicken, lamb, or doner meat (no, I don't know what it's made of either) and your choice of sauce. It is then all squashed under a toaster for a couple of minutes and then given to you in all its delicious glory. Perfect as a snack on the go or after a night enjoying what Granada has to offer.

41. INTERNATIONAL FOOD

Despite having a plethora of great Spanish food to choose from, sometimes something a bit different takes your fancy. Granada is quite a multicultural city so you can find some excellent choices for international food.

If you're looking for East Asian food there are a few decent Chinese restaurants dotted around the city. I would recommend La Estrella Oriental on Calle Álvaro de Bazán, just off Gran Vía de Colón. The food is excellent and they also have a great value daily menu if you don't want to spend too much. For incredible Japanese food, look no further than Restaurante Yamato, on Calle Colcha, just off Plaza Nueva. They also have a well-priced menú del día and their sushi is by far some of the best I've ever tasted at really reasonable prices.

For Southeast Asian food, Muglia is your best bet. Although a little more pricey, the food is of an outstanding quality and well worth it. They have two places - one on Calle Casillas de Prats, near Plaza de Gracia, and one on Calle Joaquín Costa, near Plaza Nueva.

With Spain's close proximity to Morocco, there is a good selection of Arabic and Middle Eastern food to choose from. Many of the restaurants surround the Plaza Nueva/Calle Elvira area and are quite touristy and usually overpriced. Moving away from the usually Moroccan-owned kebab places, you must check out Om-Kalsum on Calle Jardines, super popular with locals, which has a fantastic selection of Moroccan food and tapas to choose from which are made fresh to order. This place also has a good selection of vegetarian options.

For more Levantine cuisine, check out the Lebanese restaurant Samarcanda on Calle Calderería Vieja which is family run and has excellent quality, authentic food. Some of the best Syrian food can be found at Puerta de Syria on Calle Elvira. Another family run place, with excellent prices and incredible flavours.

And finally, for a really unusual twist, try Elvira 81, a lovely little place owned by a Venezuelan couple with Andalusian and Canarian roots. They freshly prepare the South American arepa, which can be made with fillings of your choice, as well as having gluten-free options. They also make fantastic natural juices and specials of the day. They also plan on selling products from the Alpujarras - Andalucía with a mix of South America - what's not to love?!

42. DISGUSTING FRUIT

As you wander through the beautifully enchanting Granadino streets, you will spot bright oranges on the trees and marvel at the fact that they're hanging there so perfectly, so ripe and ready to eat, and yet remain untouched. Even the odd stray cat and dog don't touch them; the old proverb 'curiosity killed the cat' springs to mind, and they must be aware of it in the literal sense as although the taste may not kill you, it certainly might your tastebuds.

These orange trees are only useful for one thing - to fill the warm, spring evening air with the most incredible scent of orange blossom which drifts over you when sitting on a terrace and makes you think that life can't get much better than this...

Except it can; if you want to taste some fantastic fruit with intense, full flavour and vivid colours you only see in the pictures of magazines - make your way over to any of the fruterias (fruit shop/greengrocers) scattered across the city. Most of the produce is fresh every day and brought to the city in the early hours by the vendors who then display it in a fashion to tease all your senses.

One of my favourites is Fruiteria de Abdul about half way down Calle Elvira - a small, fairly dark

place which you could easily walk past, but don't!
There is a grand variety and the produce is excellent
and fantastically priced. The owner is friendly,
welcoming and extremely helpful and will strive to
get something in for you if he doesn't have it.

43. FROG'S LEGS, PIG'S HEADS, SQUID RINGS – MARKET TIME!

For a fantastically local experience, heading to the
market is a must. The stalls are aplenty with fresh
meats, fish, bread, olives, honey, cheese, cuts of meat,
fruit and vegetables. You really will be spoilt for
choice! The beauty of shopping in the market as
opposed to the supermarket, is that you can choose
how much you want of everything instead of buying
great big bulks like the supermarkets tend to sell.

Most stalls give you little tasters before you buy so
you can decide on the bitterness of the olive or the
smoothness of the cheese to suit your palate.

The Mercado San Agustin right behind the
Cathedral has stalls selling an abundance of fruit and
vegetables for you to try. Chirimoyas (Custard
apples) are particularly popular; as well as avocados

which are cheap and delicious. Remember, in Spain most things are only available according to the season so if you're craving watermelon in November, you're going to have to make do with an apple instead.

If having the option to buy only the freshest local ingredients wasn't enough, there are also places to eat - take your pick from sushi, fresh seafood, snails, and even frog legs! This market is really like no other!

44. WINTER TREATS

In the winter months Granada is FREEZING, and the snow on the mountains surrounding the city can be spotted from across different viewpoints. Snowsports fanatics flock with glee to the Sierra Nevada, while the rest of us wonder how on earth we're going to keep warm and survive another Granadino winter without tears.

With winter come some delicacies which can't be found at other times of the year. Most notably there are small pop-up tables that appear on street corners with people roasting and selling cones of castaños (chestnuts) which you can pick up and take along with you on your crisp, chilly walks through the city.

Another favourite is turrón, a nougat sweet which is typically made with toasted almonds, honey, sugar and eggs. You can get different types - hard or soft - and a variety of flavours including chocolate, coffee, and marzipan.

Finally, polvorones - a small, round, crumbly 'biscuit' made from nuts, flour, sugar. They are quite 'heavy' in taste and have a powdery texture. There are many different varieties including some with or without alcohol. However, vegetarians beware -- polvorones are usually made with animal gelatine so they might seem like an innocent treat, but not if you prefer not to eat your furry friends.

45. THE ALPUJARRAS

Granada's most famous mountain range, the Sierra Nevada, to the southeast of the city, is home to The Alpujarras - a collection of small, white-washed mountainous villages which stand almost intact since the time of the Moors. The Alpujarras are unique in Spain and have an air of fascination about them which draw artists, travellers, and bohemian types to its small community.

As well as having unique handicrafts such as carpets, straw baskets and hats, the Alpujarras produce some great quality meats, wines, and cheese.

Thanks to the great biodiversity of the region, it is able to produce a fantastic tasting honey made from the nectar of a mixture of flowers including orange blossom, lavender, elm, and rosemary. The honey can be purchased in glass jars or alternatively, as a nice gift, it can be bought in terracotta jars which are hand painted with the words 'Miel de la Alpujarra' - Honey from the Alpujarras - a nice memento of your time here.

If you have time during your trip and you want to see a different side to Granada that isn't urban, a day trip to the Alpujarras is an absolute must. You can rent a car, catch a taxi or the bus from the bus station and get dropped off at the first main village of the area, Lanjarón, and walk up through the different villages until you get to Pampeneira, arguably one of the most beautiful of the Alpujarras.

46. TROPICAL COAST

Little known to some travellers, Granada has its own coastline less than an hour away. The Costa Tropical, or Tropical Coast can be reached by ALSA buses from the bus station (see the link at the end), or the most comfortable way is by car if you have access to one.

A big favourite with locals is El Peñón restaurant in Salobreña for the fried fish, or I would recommend Chiringuito Casa Emilio for fantastic quality and price.

For something sweeter, leche rizada is your choice. This delicious cooling dessert is made with milk, sugar and cinnamon with a flavouring of rice pudding and is proudly native to the Granadino coast. Salobreña and Motril are the places to find the best ones - Heladería Panandrés has been specialising in ice creams for over 100 years and people return summer after summer for some of their leche rizada de Motril.

47. NORTH AFRICA IN SOUTHERN SPAIN

In some parts of Granada you wouldn't be mistaken for thinking that you'd just stepped into the winding streets of Fez or Marrakech. Just behind the Cathedral and leading down to Plaza Bib-Rambla is the Alcaicería, or great bazaar of Granada. Originally the old Moorish silk market, the labyrinth of alleyways are bursting with trinkets and beautiful handicrafts for you to buy.

Many of the treasures on sale are traditionally made and so even if you never get the chance to go to Morocco, you feel like you've had an authentic introduction and have a beautiful example of Arabic craftwork to boot. In this area you will also find stalls selling a variety of Moroccan herbs, spices, dried fruit, and teas. Stock up ready to try out some new recipes from your travels when you get home.

48. CHILL OUT, RELAX MAN

Something that has become really popular in recent years with the locals are places called chill out - usually places to go after lunch at any time after 5pm. The music is relaxed and soft, there are often comfy sofas, cushions, and a general atmosphere of kick back and relax. Most people choose to have a cocktail or mocktail, but a variety of teas and coffees are also on offer as well as desserts like crêpes and cheesecakes making the atmosphere very much that of quiet and relaxation and not "let's go" wild parties.

One of the best in the centre is Monasterio Chillout located on the roof of Hotel Jerónimo on Calle San Juan de Dios. The service is excellent and it has fantastic views over the Monastery of San Jerónimo, especially in the early evening as dusk is approaching and the sky turns into a magical mixture of reds and purples.

If you prefer to try somewhere further out, take the number 33 bus out to the nearby village of Cenes de la Vega to CoffeePub Eritana (Ctra. de la Sierra, 152). Located between beautiful mountains and stunning scenery, if you're looking for a relaxed time amongst nature - this is the place for you.

49. SAY NO TO THE BIG MAN

One of the things that hit me most about Granada when I first arrived, and what I still love about it, is that it hasn't been invaded (as I like to say) by your usual fast food giants that besiege most cities around the world. You will not find one single McDonalds in the centre of Granada, that's right! Not.a.single.one. For foodies like me, this really is a dream. This means that visitors and locals alike are 'forced' to hunt out other eateries which are by far more interesting, delicious, authentic, and genuine experiences.

Not only does this support the local economy and the hundreds of small family-run restaurants and bars across the city, but it also gives you a real insight into Spanish customs, flavours, and dishes. Andalucía produces so many fresh, quality ingredients, which are used by the restaurants here, it would be a real shame to not take the opportunity whilst here to eat solely local cuisine in authentic places.

Okay, okay, so there is a Burger King right in the centre where the streets Recogidas and Reyes Católicos meet, but we'll just overlook this as it's the only one and not as glaringly obvious as a great big yellow 'M' in the skyline.

NB, Don't worry - if you can't imagine a trip without your Maccie D's hit, you can find one by the bus station, by the football ground Los Carmenes in Zaidín, and in the two main shopping centres in the city - Serrallo Plaza and Nevada Shopping. I won't judge you. Promise.

50. WALK IT!

My final tip is not quite food related - but is just as important to enjoy Granada at its best. If you are physically able to, I highly recommend walking as much as possible when in Granada. The city is relatively small and everything can be reached on foot within around 45 minutes from one end of the city to the other.

There are options to catch the tourist bus and the sightseeing train, but without a doubt the best way to see Granada is on foot. This way you can experience the sights, smells, sounds, and life that this city holds - the locals love to take a stroll around the city - especially in the early evening. Join them and enjoy Granada at its best, following your nose for choosing places to eat, taking in the pretty plazas with the birds swooping in and out of the trees, chattering excitedly.

Wandering around the side streets of the pomegranate city you are bound to come across new places to feast and quench your thirst, be ready to feed your tummy and your soul in this magical place.

HELPFUL RESOURCES

http://www.granadadirect.com/

http://www.granadadirect.com/transporte/autobuses-granada/

https://metropolitanogranada.es/

https://www.alsa.com/en/web/bus/home

https://glovoapp.com/

https://www.just-eat.es/

READ OTHER BOOKS BY CZYK PUBLISHING

Greater Than a Tourist- St. Croix US Birgin Islands USA: 50 Travel Tips from a Local by Tracy Birdsall

Greater Than a Tourist- Toulouse France: 50 Travel Tips from a Local by Alix Barnaud

Children's Book: *Charlie the Cavalier Travels the World* by Lisa Rusczyk

Eat Like a Local

Follow *Eat Like a Local on* Amazon.
Join our mailing list for new books
http://bit.ly/EatLikeaLocalbooks

Eat Like a Local